LAKE CLASSICS

**Great Short Stories
from Around the World I**

WITHDRAWN
Rabindranath
TAGORE

Stories retold by C. D. Buchanan
Illustrated by James Balkovek

LAKE EDUCATION
Belmont, California

LAKE CLASSICS

Great American Short Stories I

Washington Irving, Nathaniel Hawthorne, Mark Twain, Bret Harte, Edgar Allan Poe, Kate Chopin, Willa Cather, Sarah Orne Jewett, Sherwood Anderson, Charles W. Chesnutt

Great American Short Stories II

Herman Melville, Stephen Crane, Ambrose Bierce, Jack London, Edith Wharton, Charlotte Perkins Gilman, Frank R. Stockton, Hamlin Garland, O. Henry, Richard Harding Davis

Great British and Irish Short Stories I

Arthur Conan Doyle, Saki (H. H. Munro), Rudyard Kipling, Katherine Mansfield, Thomas Hardy, E. M. Forster, Robert Louis Stevenson, H. G. Wells, John Galsworthy, James Joyce

Great Short Stories from Around the World I

Guy de Maupassant, Anton Chekhov, Leo Tolstoy, Selma Lagerlöf, Alphonse Daudet, Mori Ogwai, Leopoldo Alas, Rabindranath Tagore, Fyodor Dostoevsky, Honoré de Balzac

Cover and Text Designer: Diann Abbott

Library of Congress Catalog Number: 94-075347
ISBN 1-56103-046-5
Printed in the United States of America
1 9 8 7 6 5 4 3 2

CONTENTS

❧ Lake Classic Short Stories ❧

"The universe is made of stories, not atoms."
    —Muriel Rukeyser

"The story's about you."
    —Horace

Everyone loves a good story. It is hard to think of a friendlier introduction to classic literature. For one thing, short stories are *short*—quick to get into and easy to finish. Of all the literary forms, the short story is the least intimidating and the most approachable.

Great literature is an important part of our human heritage. In the belief that this heritage belongs to everyone, *Lake Classic Short Stories* are adapted for today's readers. Lengthy sentences and paragraphs are shortened. Archaic words are replaced. Modern punctuation and spellings are used. Many of the longer stories are abridged. In all the stories, painstaking care has been taken to preserve the author's unique voice.

Lake Classic Short Stories have something for everyone. The hundreds of stories in the collection cover a broad terrain of themes, story types, and styles. Literary merit was a deciding factor in story selection. But no story was included unless it was as enjoyable as it was instructive. And special priority was given to stories that shine light on the human condition.

Each book in the *Lake Classic Short Stories* is devoted to the work of a single author. Little-known stories of merit are included with famous old favorites. Taken as a whole, the collected authors and stories make up a rich and diverse sampler of the story-teller's art.

Lake Classic Short Stories guarantee a great reading experience. Readers who look for common interests, concerns, and experiences are sure to find them. Readers who bring their own gifts of perception and appreciation to the stories will be doubly rewarded.

❧ Rabindranath Tagore ❧
(1861–1941)

About the Author

Rabindranath Tagore was born in Calcutta, India. The Tagores were a famous family of artists, musicians, and social reformers. The boy was brought up in a literary atmosphere. He began writing Bengali lyrics at an early age.

Young Tagore greatly admired the English poets Shelley and Keats. He was 16 when he visited England for the first time. It would be 35 years before he returned. This time he brought with him an English translation of *Gitānjali*, a collection of his poetry. Its greatness was immediately recognized. Published in 1913, the work established Tagore's international reputation.

Tagore received the Nobel prize in 1913, and he was knighted by King George V in 1914. (In an interesting footnote to history, Tagore resigned his knighthood in 1919. This he did to protest Britain's oppression of Indians in the Punjab.)

Tagore was a true "man of all arts." In addition to the lyrical poems that made him famous, he wrote essays, novels, and short stories. Many of his poems were set to music. His "dance dramas" adapted the techniques of opera to the Bengali stage. In his last years he became an accomplished painter. His symbolic paintings were praised by one critic as "vivid and rich."

And Tagore was also an educator. In 1901 he founded a "world university" about 100 miles from Calcutta. This famous school was called *Shantiniketan*, Indian for "The Abode of Peace." Tagore's goal was to give Indian boys a retreat from the modern world where they could be taught traditional ideals.

The four charming stories that you are about to read were translated from the original Bengali in 1918.

The Castaway

Do you believe that a person is innocent until proven guilty? A husband and wife disagree about a homeless boy. The wife loves him but the husband is suspicious. What's the truth about Nilkanta?

THE BOY'S NARROW ESCAPE FROM DEATH TOUCHED
KIRAN'S HEART.

The Castaway

Towards evening the storm was at its height. A battle between the gods and demons seemed to be raging in the skies. Thunder crashed and lightning flashed. There was a terrific downpour of rain. The Ganges River was lashed into a fury. In the gardens along the riverbanks, the wind blew the trees from side to side.

Beside the river, a husband and wife were staying in one of the great houses, or villas. They were having a discussion inside a closed room. An earthen lamp burned beside them.

The husband, Sharat, was saying, "I wish you would stay here a few more days. By then you would be strong enough to return home."

The wife, Kiran, was saying, "I have recovered already. It can't do me any harm to go home now."

Like a boat without a rudder, the discussion seemed to be going round and round. At last it threatened to end in a flood of tears.

Sharat said, "It is not only I who say so. The doctor thinks you should stay here a few days longer."

Kiran replied, "I suppose your doctor knows everything!"

Kiran was a great favorite with her family and neighbors. When she became seriously ill, they were all very worried. So Sharat and his mother took their little darling to Chandernagore. They thought that a change of air would help her to get well.

And Kiran did indeed recover at Chandernagore—though she was still very weak. There was a pinched look on her face. Her family could not forget how narrowly she had escaped death. They were still worried about her.

Kiran loved all people and most amusements. Life in a riverside villa was lonely for her. She did not like it. There was nothing to do. There were no interesting neighbors. She hated to spend all day fussing with medicines. It was no fun to be here. This was what Kiran and Sharat were discussing this stormy evening.

As long as Kiran would argue, Sharat thought there was a chance of a fair fight. But sometimes she refused to reply. When she tossed her head and looked the other way, her poor husband was defeated. This point had arrived. Sharat was about to give in to her when a servant shouted through the closed door.

Sharat opened the door. The servant told him that a boat had been upset in the storm. One of its passengers was a young boy. He had swum ashore in their garden, the servant said as he roughly pushed the boy forward.

At once, Kiran turned back into her own sweet self. She got dry clothes for the boy. She then warmed a cup of milk and invited him to her room.

The boy had long curly hair and big, expressive eyes. Kiran asked the boy to tell her all about himself.

He told her that his name was Nilkanta. He said that he belonged to a troupe of traveling actors. When the storm began, they were coming to put on a show in a nearby villa. But then their boat was overturned. The boy had no idea what had become of the other actors. Lucky for him he was quite a good swimmer. Yet, even so, he had just barely managed to reach shore.

The boy stayed on with them. His narrow escape from a terrible death touched Kiran's soft heart. She took a warm interest in him. Sharat too was pleased that the boy had turned up. Now his wife had something to amuse her, she might stay on longer.

Kiran's mother-in-law was also quite pleased. And the boy Nilkanta himself was delighted. Not only had he escaped from death, but also from his cruel master. And he had found himself a comfortable home with a rich family!

In a short while, however, Sharat and his mother changed their minds. Both of them longed for the boy to leave. He smoked Sharat's pipes. Without asking, he took Sharat's best umbrella out in the rain. Everyone he met in the village became his friend. He even brought home a village dog that came indoors with muddy paws. In just a few days, the boy rounded up a devoted band of boys from the village. They stripped the mango trees bare in all the villa gardens.

There was no doubt that Kiran had a hand in spoiling the boy. Sharat often warned her about it—but she would not listen to him. She made a dandy of him with Sharat's cast-off clothes. And she gave him new ones, too. Kiran was curious to know more about the boy. Every day she called him to her own room. In the afternoons, Kiran had Nilkanta recite pieces from the plays that he knew. Sometimes she tried to persuade Sharat to be one of the audience. But Sharat strongly disliked the boy by then. He always refused. Sometimes his mother would come, but usually she fell asleep.

Sharat often boxed Nilkanta's ears for his pranks. But this was nothing to the boy. Compared to the rough treatment he had known in the acting company,

Sharat's punishments were soft. The boy had learned long ago that life was made up of nothing but eatings and beatings. Mostly beatings.

It was hard to tell Nilkanta's age. If it was only 14 or 15, then his face was too old for his years. But if he was 17 or 18 years old, his face was too young. He was either a man too early or a boy too late. His beard had not begun to grow, and he was small. So he looked quite young and innocent.

In the shelter of Sharat's house and garden, Nilkanta began to mature. His feelings began to catch up with his age. When Kiran treated him like a boy, it made him feel ashamed. And now, when she called for him to act out his old parts, he ran off.

He tried learning to read, but the alphabet did a misty dance before his eyes. He never could keep going from one word to another. Yet sometimes he sat for hours with an open book on his lap. What thoughts passed through his mind as he looked at it, he alone knew.

Shortly after the arrival of Nilkanta, Sharat's younger brother had also arrived. Satish had come to spend his college vacation with his family. Kiran was very pleased at finding a fresh new amusement. She and Satish were the same age. They spent hours together in games and quarrels and laughter and even tears. They constantly played jokes on each other. The house rang with their peals of laughter.

Meanwhile, Nilkanta's heart became filled with bitterness. He felt that he must avenge his anger on somebody or something. Sometimes he would beat up his boy-followers and send them away crying. At other times he would kick his dog until it howled. When he went out for a walk, he would beat the bushes with his cane.

Kiran was spending most of her time with Satish. Now she no longer shared meals with Nilkanta. Without her to urge him to try this and that, the poor boy was miserable. Nothing tasted right. Every day he would get up from the table without eating much. "I am not hungry," he would say. Nilkanta hoped that news of this would reach Kiran. He hoped that she would send for him and urge him to eat more. But nothing of the sort ever happened. Kiran never knew, and never sent for him. Night after night Nilkanta would throw himself on his bed and cry himself to sleep.

Nilkanta blamed Satish. As he thought it over, he came to believe that Satish was poisoning Kiran's mind against him. When he heard Satish laughing with his sister-in-law, fury burned in his heart.

Nilkanta never dared to show his anger openly. But he would find a hundred little ways to torment Satish. When Satish went for a swim in the river, he would find his soap gone when he returned. Once he found his favorite tunic floating past him on the water. He thought it had been blown away by a strong gust of wind.

Then one day Kiran sent for Nilkanta. She wanted him to recite for Satish. But Nilkanta stood there in gloomy silence. That was quite a surprise to Kiran. She asked him what was the matter. But the boy remained silent. And when she again asked him to repeat a favorite piece of hers, he refused. "I don't remember," he said, and walked away.

At last the time came for Sharat and Kiran to return to their own home. Everybody was busy packing up. Satish was going with them. But to Nilkanta, nobody said a word. No one seemed to have thought about what would happen to the boy.

But as a matter of fact, the question *had* been raised by Kiran. She proposed to take him along with them. But her husband and his mother and brother had all objected. She had let the matter drop. A few days before they were to start, she sent for the boy. With kind words she advised him to go back to his own home.

Nilkanta had felt neglected for so long that her kindness was too much for him. He burst into tears. Kiran's eyes were also brimming over. Now she was very sad that she had created a bond that could not last.

But Satish was very annoyed at the blubbering of this overgrown boy. "Why does the fool stand there howling instead of speaking?" he asked. Kiran scolded him. She said that he was a hard, unfeeling creature.

"Sister of mine," her brother-in-law

replied, "you do not understand. You are much too good and trustful. This fellow turned up from heaven knows where. And you treated him like a king! Naturally he has no wish to return to his old life. He knows very well that his tears will soften your heart."

Nilkanta hurriedly left the room. He wished for a knife to cut Satish to pieces. He wished for a needle to pierce the man through and through. He wished a fire would burn him to ashes. But Satish was not even wounded. It was Nilkanta's own heart that bled.

Satish had brought a beautiful inkstand with him on his visit. The inkpot was in a mother-of-pearl boat drawn by a silver goose. This inkstand was a great favorite of his.

The day before Sharat and Kiran were to begin their journey, the inkstand was missing. It could be found nowhere.

Kiran smiled at her brother-in-law. "Your goose has flown off to find you a wife," she teased.

But Satish was in a great rage. He was certain that Nilkanta had stolen it. Several people said they had seen the boy prowling about the room the night before. So Satish had Nilkanta brought before him. Kiran was also there.

"You have stolen my inkstand, you thief!" he blurted out. To be called a thief in Kiran's presence was more than Nilkanta could stand. His eyes blazed with a wild anger. His throat choked. If Satish had said another word, he would have flown at him like a wild cat.

The scene upset Kiran. She took the boy into another room. In her sweet, kind way she spoke to him. "Nilu," she said, "if you really have taken that inkstand— give it to me quietly. I shall see that no one says another word to you about it."

Big tears ran down the boy's cheeks. He hid his face in his hands and wept. Kiran came back from the room. "I am sure that Nilkanta has not taken the inkstand," she said. But Sharat and Satish did not believe it. They were sure that only Nilkanta could have done it.

But Kiran said, "Never."

Sharat wanted to ask the boy more questions, but his wife would not allow another word to be said about it.

Then Satish said that the boy's room and trunk should be searched. That made Kiran very angry. "If you do such a thing," she said, "I will never forgive you. No! You shall not spy on this poor, innocent boy!"

And as she spoke, her wonderful eyes filled with tears. That settled the matter.

Kiran's heart overflowed with pity for the homeless lad. She bought two new suits of clothes and a pair of shoes for

him. With these gifts and some money
in her hand, she quietly went into
Nilkanta's room. She meant to put these
presents into his trunk as a surprise. The
trunk itself had also been her gift.

She opened the trunk. It was so full
that the new clothes would not go in! She
took everything out so she could pack the
trunk properly. At first she found odds
and ends like knives and tops—things
dear to every boy's heart. Then came a
layer of underwear. At the bottom of the
trunk was the missing inkstand!

Kiran sat down with the inkstand in
her hand. For a long time she sat there,
puzzled and wondering.

In the meantime, Nilkanta had come
into the room. He had seen the whole
thing. He thought that Kiran had come
like a thief to catch him in his thieving.
Now how could he ever convince her
otherwise? In his heart he knew that he

had never really been a thief.

It was only his desire for revenge that made him take the inkstand. He had meant to throw it into the river. But in a moment of weakness, he had put it in his trunk. *"I am not a thief!"* his heart cried out. But then—what was he? What could he say? He had stolen, and yet he was not a thief! How could he explain to Kiran that she was wrong about him? And how could he bear the thought that she had spied on him?

Sighing deeply, Kiran replaced the inkstand in the trunk. As if she were the thief herself, she covered it up as it was before. In the top of the trunk she placed the presents and the money.

The next day the boy was nowhere to be found. The villagers had not seen him. The police could find no trace of him. "Now let us have a look at his trunk," Sharat said. But Kiran would not allow it. She had a servant bring the trunk to her own room. Taking out the inkstand, she threw it into the river.

The whole family went home. The house and garden were empty. Only that starving dog of Nilkanta's remained. Now it prowled along the river bank, whining and whining as if its heart would break.

The Skeleton

Do you believe in spirits? In this story a talkative ghost disturbs a man's sleep. What memories does she share about her life on earth?

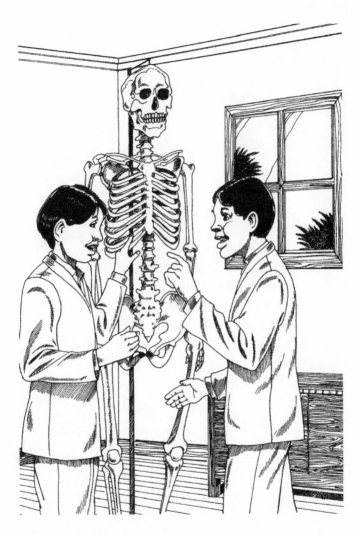

IN THE NIGHT THE SKELETON WOULD RATTLE IN THE
BREEZE. IN THE DAY IT WOULD BE RATTLED BY US.

The Skeleton

The bedroom in which we boys used to sleep had a smaller room next to it. In that little room hung a human skeleton. In the night it would rattle in the breeze. In the day the bones were rattled by us. A medical student was giving us lessons in the study of bones. Our guardians had hired him to teach us about the human body. They were determined to make us masters of all the sciences.

Many years have passed since then. In the meantime the skeleton has vanished from that little room. Our knowledge of bones has also vanished from our brains.

The other day, our house was crowded with guests. I had to spend the night in the same old room. Sleep refused to come, and I tossed from side to side. I heard the clock chime each hour, one after another. Finally, after some spluttering, the lamp went out.

We had recently had several deaths in our family. Naturally, the going out of the lamp led me to thoughts of death. I thought about the light of the lamp losing itself in darkness. It seemed much the same as the going out of our little human lives.

My mournful thoughts of the past made me remember the skeleton. I tried to imagine what the body that had covered it might have looked like. Then suddenly it seemed to me that something was walking round and round my bed. I could hear its rapid breathing. It seemed to be searching for something. The restless pacing got faster and faster. I was sure that this sound was a fancy of my sleepless brain. Nevertheless, I felt a cold shiver.

"Who is there?" I called out. The footsteps seemed to stop at my bedside. "It is I," came the reply. "I have come to look for my skeleton."

It seemed silly to be afraid of a dream creature. So I said in a casual sort of way, "Well! A nice business for this time of night! Of what use will that skeleton be to you now?"

The reply seemed to come from the bed curtain itself. "What a question! In that skeleton are the bones that once encircled my heart. The youth and beauty of my 26 years bloomed about that skeleton. Should I not desire to see it once more?"

"Of course," said I. "That is a perfectly

reasonable desire. Go on with your search, by all means. In the meantime, I'll try to get a little sleep."

"But I think that you must be lonely," said the voice. "I'll sit down a while, and we will have a little chat. Years ago I often sat by men and talked with them. But for the last 35 years, I have only moaned in the wind. It would be nice to talk with a living man again."

I felt that someone sat down just beside my curtain. I gave up trying to sleep. "Very well," I said. "Let us talk of something cheerful."

"The funniest thing I can think of is my own life story. "Let me tell it to you."

The clock chimed the hour of two.

"When I was a young woman in the land of the living, I feared one thing like death itself. That was my husband. My feelings were like those of a fish caught on a hook. He snatched me from the peace of my childhood home. I had no way to escape from him.

"Then just two months after my marriage, my husband died. Then my husband's father said to my mother-in-law, 'Look! Do you not see? She has the evil eye.' Well—are you listening? I hope you are enjoying the story?"

"Very much indeed!" I said. "The beginning is certainly very funny."

"Let me go on then. I came back to my father's house in great happiness. In those days I had a rare and radiant beauty. People tried to conceal it from me, but I was very aware of it. What is your opinion?"

"Very likely," I murmured. "But you must remember that I have never seen you before."

"What! Not seen me? What about that skeleton of mine? Ha! ha! ha! Never mind. I was only joking. How can I ever make you believe the truth? That in those two hollows shone the brightest of dark eyes? And that the smile of my ruby lips was truly glorious? In no way did my smile look like the grinning teeth that you boys used to see.

"It makes me smile to remember the grace, the charm, the dimples and curves, that once blossomed over those dry old bones. It also makes me angry. No doctors of my day would have dreamed of doing such a thing. To use my bones as teaching material! One young doctor actually compared me to a *champack* blossom. And does anyone think of the skeleton of a flower?

"I had no girl companions at all," the voice went on. "My only brother had decided not to marry. I used to sit in the garden dreaming that the whole world was in love with me. It seemed to me that all the young men in the world were at my feet. They were like the very blades of grass. My heart—I know not why—used to grow sad.

"When my brother's good friend, Shekhar, finished medical college, he became our family doctor. I had seen him often from behind a curtain. My brother was a strange man. He did not care for the world. He gradually moved away from it until he was quite lost in a corner. Shekhar was his one friend. He was the only young man I ever got to see. So when I sat in the garden, I imagined that all the young men at my feet were Shekhar." She paused. "Are you listening? What are you thinking of?"

I sighed before I answered. "I was wishing I was Shekhar!"

"Wait a bit. Hear the whole story first. One day, in the rains, I was quite feverish. The doctor came to see me. That was our first meeting. I was lying down by the window. The pink of the evening sky shone on me. When the doctor looked into my face, I gazed at myself in my imagination. I saw my delicate face resting like a flower against the pillow. My curls fell over my forehead. My lowered eyelids cast a soft shadow on my cheeks.

"The doctor asked my brother, 'Might I feel her pulse?'

"I put out a smooth, well-rounded wrist from beneath the coverlet. I have never before seen a doctor so awkward about feeling a patient's pulse. His fingers trembled. He measured the heat of my fever. I measured the pulse of his heart. Don't you believe me?"

"Very easily," said I. "The human heartbeat tells its tale."

"I was very ill, but I was able to recover several times. After that, there remained in my little world only one doctor and one patient.

"In those evenings I used to secretly dress myself in a yellow dress. It had to be done secretly, because widows are supposed to dress in white only. I would twine into my hair a garland of white jasmine blossoms. I took a little mirror in my hand. Then I would go to my usual seat under the trees.

"Well! Are you thinking that the sight of one's own beauty would soon grow boring? Ah, no! For I did not see myself with my own eyes. I used to see myself with the doctor's eyes. I gazed, I was charmed. I fell madly in love.

"From that time on, I was never alone. Always I saw myself as if I were the doctor. My dainty little toes, my elegant hands—all that beauty I saw with his eyes! Always I imagined him with me.

"What if I ended the story here? How would it do?"

"Not too bad an ending," I replied thoughtfully. "But it would be somewhat *incomplete*, wouldn't it? I suppose, however, that I could add the finishing touches myself."

"But that would make the story too serious. Where would the laugh come in? Where would that leave the skeleton with its grinning teeth?

"So let me go on. Over time, the doctor built up a small practice. Then he took a room in our house for an office. I used to ask him jokingly about medicines and poisons. I asked how much of this drug or that would kill a man. He liked the subject and he would talk away. In this way I grew familiar with the idea of death. So thoughts of love and death were the only two things that filled my little world. My story is now nearly ended. There is not much left."

"Not very much of the night is left, either," I muttered.

"After a time I noticed that the doctor

had grown strangely absent-minded. It seemed as if he were ashamed of something. I felt that he was trying to keep it from me. Then one day he came in, very smartly dressed. He borrowed my brother's carriage for the evening.

"My curiosity was too great to bear. I went to my brother for information. After some chit-chat, I at last came to the point. 'I see that the doctor is using your carriage. Where is he going this evening?'

"My brother replied briefly. 'To his death,' he said.

"'Oh, do tell me,' I begged. 'Where is he *really* going?'

"'To be married,' he said.

"'Oh, indeed!' I said in disbelief. I laughed long and loudly.

"Then I learned that the bride was very rich. The marriage would bring the doctor a large sum of money. But why did he insult me by hiding his plans? Had

I ever begged him not to marry? Had I ever said that my heart would break if he married? Men are not to be trusted. I had known only one man in my life, and I found this out in a second.

"When the doctor came in after his work, I spoke up. 'Well, doctor, so you are to be married tonight?' I was laughing as I spoke.

"My gaiety irritated the doctor.

"'How is it,' I went on, 'that there are no lights, no music?'

"He sighed. Then he replied, 'Do you think marriage is always such a joyful occasion?'

"I burst out laughing again. 'No, no,' I said. 'This will never do. Who ever heard of a wedding without lights and music?'

"I scolded my brother until he ordered everything for a wedding.

"All the time I kept on happily talking about the bride. I talked about what I would do when she came home. 'And doctor,' I asked, 'will you still go on feeling pulses?' Ha! ha! ha! I can swear that my words were piercing the doctor's heart like deadly darts.

"The marriage was to take place late at night. Before the ceremony, the doctor and my brother were having a glass of wine together. This was their daily habit. The moon had just risen over the terrace.

"I went up to the doctor, smiling. 'Have you forgotten your wedding, doctor?' I said. 'It is time to start.'

"Oh, I almost forgot! I must tell you one more little thing. Just before that I had gone down to the doctor's office and got a little powder. Already I had dropped it into the doctor's glass, when he wasn't looking.

"The doctor drank his wine at one gulp. With a look that tore my heart, he said, 'Then I must go.'

"The music struck up. I went into my room and dressed myself in bridal robes of silk and gold. I put on all my jewelry. And then, under the tree in the garden, I prepared my bed.

"It was a beautiful night. The scent of jasmine filled the air.

"The sound of the music began to grow fainter. The light of the moon grew dimmer. Then I closed my eyes and smiled to myself.

"I imagined what would happen when people found me. The first thing they would see was that smile. It would linger on my lips like a trace of rose wine. When I entered my eternal bridal chamber, I would carry that smile with me. It would light up my face. But alas for the bridal chamber! Alas for the bridal robes of silk and gold! I awoke at the sound of a rattling within me. I found three brats were studying the bones of my skeleton.

Where my heart used to beat, and my joys and griefs used to throb, there was the teacher with his pointer! He was busy naming my bones. And as to that last smile—did you see any sign of it?"

I was silent for a moment.

"Well, well, how did you like the story?"

"It has been quite delightful," I said truthfully.

Then at this point, the first crow began to caw. "Are you there?" I asked. There was no reply.

Morning light entered the room.

My Fair Neighbor

Have you ever encouraged a friend's romance? In this story a poet helps his shy friend write love verses. Why isn't he happy when the courtship succeeds?

My friend Nabin was struck by an urge to write verse. He came to me for help.

My Fair Neighbor

I had feelings for the young widow who lived in the house next to mine. I told my friends and myself that these were feelings of respect. Even my best friend, Nabin, knew nothing of my secret feelings. I felt rather proud that I could hide my real feelings deep in my heart. It kept my love pure for this beautiful flower of a woman. She was far too lovely—even too holy—for marriage. She seemed to belong to heaven itself.

But passion is like a mountain stream. Unwilling to be pent up, it seeks a way out. That is why I tried to pour my feelings into my poems. But my pen refused to write about my beloved. She was too pure even for poetry!

Just at this time, my friend Nabin was struck by an urge to write verse. It came upon him like an earthquake. It was the poor fellow's first attack. He didn't know how to manage it. Unable to control himself, he wrote away madly. But he knew nothing about rhyme or rhythm. So he came to me for help.

The subject of his poems was the old, old one, which is ever new. Every one of his verses was written to "the beloved." I laughed. "Well, old chap, who is she?" I asked him.

Nabin laughed, too. "I have not yet discovered who she is," he replied with a twinkle in his eye.

I must say that it comforted me to help my friend. I felt like a hen on the nest.

Nearly clucking, I poured all the warmth of my own great passion into Nabin's poems. In the end, I worked so hard to improve his poems that they in fact became mine.

When he read them, Nabin would cry out in surprise. "That is just what I wanted to say, but could not. How on earth do you do it?"

Like all poets, I would try to be modest. "My thoughts come from my imagination," I said. "As you know, truth is silent. It is the imagination which finds words. Reality holds back the flow of feeling. But imagination carves out a path for itself."

Then the poor, puzzled Nabin would agree. "Y-e-s, I see. Yes, of course." But his face looked very confused.

I have already said that I could not express my own love in words. My feelings of reverence for the beautiful widow were too strong. But with Nabin to screen my feelings, there was nothing to hold back my pen. My own love gushed out into his poems.

At times Nabin could see how much of his work was mine. He would say, "But these are yours! Let me publish them, and sign your name to them!"

"Nonsense!" I would reply, trying to spare his feelings. "These are *yours*, my dear fellow. I have only added a touch or two here and there."

Gradually, Nabin came to believe it.

Meanwhile, I sometimes turned my eyes toward the house next door. I felt like an astronomer gazing into the starry heavens. Once in a while I would catch a glimpse of my beloved. Then the pure light of her face stilled my troubled heart at once.

But one day I was startled. Could I believe my eyes? It was a hot summer afternoon. A storm was coming. In the strange light of the dark clouds, my fair neighbor stood. She was sadly gazing out into empty space. What a world of sadness and longing I saw in those beautiful black eyes! Surely that look of yearning was seeking—not heaven—but the nest of some human heart!

The sight of the passion in her look moved me deeply. Now I was no longer satisfied with helping Nabin with his poems. Now I longed to express my own passion in some worthy cause. At last I thought of something. I would work to make remarriage for widows popular in my country. And I would do more than just speak and write for my cause. I would also spend money on it.

Nabin began to argue with me about it. "Permanent widowhood is noble," he said. "It has a sense of purity and peace. Remarriage would certainly destroy this divine beauty."

Now this sort of argument always makes me furious. It makes me think of a well-fed man who tells his starving brother to feast on the songs of birds.

In a sudden burst of anger I cried out, "Nonsense! It is all very well for *you* to talk of purity and peace. You are not a widow. Do you not believe that a widow has a human heart? Is it nothing to you that a widow's heart may be throbbing with pain and desire?"

Then, to my surprise, my little speech changed Nabin's mind. After a single, thoughtful sigh, he completely agreed with what I had said. I had been far more convincing than even I knew!

After about a week, Nabin came again to ask for my help. He announced that he was getting ready to marry a young widow himself!

I was overjoyed. I hugged him and promised to give him any money that he might need. Then Nabin told me the story behind his surprising news.

I learned that Nabin's beloved was not an imaginary being. Like me, Nabin had for some time adored a widow from afar. He had not spoken of his feelings to anyone. But then he published a few of his poems, or rather *my* poems, in a magazine. These had reached the fair one. And the beauty of the poetry had moved her.

Nabin explained that he had not intended for this to happen. In fact, he had no idea that the widow could read. He had sent the magazine to her brother. This was because any member of the beloved's family is special to the lover.

In time the poet got to know the widow's brother. They often talked about the poems. Sometimes the widow herself shared in these discussions!

I had given Nabin courage when I argued against permanent widowhood. He proposed marriage to the widow. At first she refused. But then he begged—using all of my words! He even added a tear or two of his own. At last the fair one gave in. Now her guardian wanted money for the wedding arrangements.

"Take it to him at once," I said.

"But," Nabin went on, "my father has stopped my allowance. What are we to live on?" I wrote him a check at once. Then I said, "Now you must tell me who she is! Do not fear that I will be a rival. I would never do that."

"I could not tell you before," Nabin said. "She asked me not to say a word to my friends. As you know, it is very unusual for a widow to remarry. But now that all is settled, I may speak. She lives at Number 19, in the house just next to yours."

If my poor heart had been an iron boiler, it would have burst. "So she does not object to remarriage?" I asked him as simply and quietly as I could.

"Not any more," replied Nabin with a smile.

"And was it the poems alone that changed her mind?"

"Well, my poems *were* pretty good," said Nabin, modestly. "Didn't you think so, my friend?"

In my mind, I let out a scream.

But at whom was I to scream? At him? At myself? At Fate? All the same, I screamed.

The Auspicious Vision

Do you believe in love at first sight? In this story a wealthy widower spots the girl of his dreams. What surprise awaits him on their wedding day?

THE FRESH, SIMPLE FACE AMONG THE REEDS MADE A
MAGICAL PICTURE IN KANTI'S MIND.

The Auspicious Vision

Kantichandra was still a young man. Yet he did not remarry after his wife's death. Instead he spent all of his time hunting. Tall and slender, Kantichandra was a handsome fellow. All his movements were quick and graceful. He had keen eyesight and was an expert shot. He never missed his mark.

It was spring, and Kanti had gone out shooting. Many of his sporting friends came with him. They were all in boats, on a swamp. Their army of servants was also in boats. That made it impossible for the village women to bathe or to get water. All day long, the land and water trembled with the firing of the hunters' guns. Every evening the tunes of the musicians killed any chance of sleep.

One morning Kanti was seated in his boat. He was cleaning his favorite gun when suddenly he jumped. He thought he heard the cry of wild duck. Looking up, he saw a village maiden coming to the water's edge. She held two white ducklings in her arms. The little stream was hardly moving. Many weeds choked the current. The girl put the birds into the water and watched them anxiously. She seemed to be worried about the presence of the sportsmen.

Kanti noticed that the girl had a rare, fresh beauty. It was hard to guess her age. She had the figure of a young woman, but her face was still childish. It seemed that the world had left no mark there. She seemed not to know herself that she had reached young womanhood.

Kanti's gun-cleaning stopped for a while. He could not take his eyes off the girl. He had never expected to see such a face in such a spot. And yet its beauty was more perfect here than it would have been in a palace. Is it not said that a bud is lovelier on the branch than it is in a golden vase?

That day the blossoming reeds were glittering in the morning sun. The fresh, simple face among the reeds made a magical picture in Kanti's mind. As he gazed at her, the maiden jumped up in terror. She took back her ducks quickly, and gave a little cry of pain. In another moment she had left the riverbank and disappeared into the bamboo.

Looking round, Kanti saw one of his men pointing a gun at the wild ducks.

At once he rushed up to the man, tore away his gun, and gave him a slap. The astonished sportsman ended up on the ground. Then Kanti calmly went on cleaning his gun.

But Kanti's curiosity would not let him rest. He went back to the bamboo wood where he had last seen the girl. Pushing his way through, he found himself in the yard of a pleasant house. On one side was a row of barns. On the other was a clean cow-shed. The girl was seated under a flowering bush that grew nearby. Kanti saw that she was sobbing over a wounded dove. From the wet corner of her jacket, she was trying to wring a little water. This she coaxed into the bird's yellow beak. A gray cat stood with its paws on her knee. It too was looking eagerly at the bird. Every now and then, she gave the cat a warning tap on the nose.

This little picture, set in the simple country yard, charmed Kanti's heart.

The light and shade flickered through the leaves. Soft shadows danced on the girl's lap. Not far away a cow lazily switched its tail to wave off the flies. The north wind whispered softly in the bamboo. Kanti thought that she, who had looked like the Forest Queen on the riverbank, now looked like the Divine Housewife. Holding his gun, he now felt out of place. He longed to explain that it was not he who had hurt the dove. He stood wondering how he should begin. Then he heard someone calling "Sudha!" from the house. The girl jumped up. "Sudha!" the voice called out again. She took up her dove and ran inside.

"Sudha," thought Kanti to himself. "That is the word for flower nectar, or a delicious sweet drink! What a perfect name!"

Kanti returned to the boat and gave his gun to his servant. Then he went back to the front door of the house. There he found a gentleman of middle age, seated on a bench outside. The man had a peaceful face and was reading a religious book. Kanti could see in this kindly, thoughtful face something of the sweet tenderness that shone in the face of the lovely young maiden.

Kanti bowed and said, "May I ask for some water, sir? I am very thirsty." The older man welcomed him with a smile. He offered him a seat on the bench. Then he went back inside and returned with a plate of cookies and a pitcher of water. After Kanti had eaten and drunk, the gentleman begged him to introduce himself. Kanti gave his own name, his father's name, and the address of his home. Then he said, "If I can be of any service to you, sir, I shall think myself fortunate." This was the custom.

"I need no service from you, my son," said Nabin Banerji. "I have only one care at the moment."

"What is that, sir?" said Kanti.

"It is my daughter, Sudha. She is growing up." This made Kanti smile as he thought of her childish face. "I have not yet been able to find a worthy bridegroom for her," the man went on. "If I could only see her well married, I would be happy. But there is no suitable bridegroom here. And how can I possibly leave my lands to go out searching for a husband? I am far too busy."

"Please come and see me in my boat, sir," Kanti said. "Then we can have a talk about the marriage of your daughter." With these words, Kanti bowed and took his leave. Then he sent some of his men into the village to ask about the gentleman's daughter. The men heard nothing but praise for the girl's beauty and goodness.

The next day the old man came to the boat on his promised visit. Kanti bowed very low and begged the hand of his daughter for himself. The old man was overwhelmed. He had never dreamed of such good luck! Not only did Kanti belong to a fine family, but he was also the owner of much land and great riches. He could hardly open his mouth to speak. The old man thought there might be some mistake. "Can it be that a man like you desires to marry my daughter?" he asked.

"If you are willing to give her to me," said Kanti.

"Do you mean Sudha?" the man asked again.

"Yes," was the reply.

"But will you not first see and speak to her—?"

Kanti pretended that he had not seen her already. "Oh, we shall do that at the moment of the Auspicious Vision."

In India the Auspicious Vision is a very important part of the wedding ceremony.

It is the moment when the bride and bridegroom first see each other after becoming engaged.

The old man's voice shook with feeling as he answered. "My Sudha is indeed a good girl. She is well skilled in all the household arts. You are most generous to take her on trust. May she never cause you a moment's regret! This is my blessing!"

A beautiful mansion was borrowed for the wedding ceremony. Kanti did not wish to delay, so a date was set right away. At the appointed time, the bridegroom arrived on his elephant. With drums and music and many blazing torches, the ceremony began.

The time came for the Auspicious Vision. The bridal couple were covered with a red screen. Kanti looked up at his bride. Her sweet, bashful face was downcast. She wore a formal wedding headdress and her face was painted with sandal paste. He could not recognize the village maiden he had seen before. He was so overcome with strong feelings that a mist seemed to cloud his eyes.

After the wedding ceremony was over, the guests all gathered in the bridal chamber. An old village woman insisted that Kanti himself remove his wife's veil. As he did so, he jumped back.

It was not the same girl!

Something rose in his chest and seemed to pierce his brain. The light of the lamps seemed to grow dim. It was as if darkness had fallen over the face of the bride herself.

At first he felt angry with his father-in-law. Had he not shown Kanti one girl and married him to another? But then Kanti remembered that the old man had not shown him any daughter at all. This was all his own fault. Now he thought it best not to show his foolishness to the world. So he took his place again as calmly as he could.

Kanti could swallow his medicine— but he could not get rid of its taste. Now he could not bear the merry-making of the crowd. He was furious with himself as well as with everybody else.

The bride was seated beside him. Suddenly he felt her give a little start. Then she cried out loudly. A rabbit had scampered into the room and brushed across her feet. Right behind it followed the girl Kanti had seen before. She caught the rabbit up in her arms. Then she began to stroke the animal and murmur softly.

"Oh, that mad girl!" cried the women. They made signs to her that she should leave the room. But she paid no attention to them. Instead, she came up to the wedded pair. She looked into their faces

with childish curiosity. When a servant
came to lead her away, Kanti stopped her.
"Let the girl be," he said.

"What is your name?" he asked the girl
with the rabbit in her arms.

The girl gave no reply. All the women
in the room began to giggle.

Then Kanti asked another question.
"Have those little ducklings of yours
grown up yet?"

The girl stared at him blankly, just as
before.

The bewildered Kanti screwed up his
courage for another try. Tenderly he
asked about the wounded dove. Just as
before, the girl only looked at him. The
laughter in the room grew louder. At last
someone told Kanti that the girl could
neither speak nor hear. Only the animals
and birds were her true and special
friends. So it was only by chance that she
had looked up when the name of Sudha
was called.

Kanti now received a second shock. A black cloud lifted from before his eyes. With a sigh of great relief, he looked again into the face of his bride. Then came the true Auspicious Vision. The light of the lamps fell on her lovely face. So too did the light from his heart shine on her now. At this moment, he saw her true beauty shining forth. It was then he knew that Nabin's blessing would be fulfilled.

Thinking About
the Stories

The Castaway

1. All the events in a story are arranged in a certain order, or sequence. Tell about one event from the beginning of this story, one from the middle, and one from the end. How are these events related?

2. Suppose this story had a completely different outcome. Can you think of another effective ending for this story?

3. The plot is the series of events that takes place in a story. Usually, story events are linked in some way. Can you name an event in this story that was the cause of a later event?

The Skeleton

1. All stories fit into one or more categories. Is this story serious or funny? Would you call it an adventure, a love story, or a mystery? Is it a character study? Or is it simply a picture the author has painted of a certain time and place? Explain your thinking.

2. Who is the main character in this story? Who are one or two of the minor characters? Describe each of these characters in one or two sentences.

3. Some stories are packed with action. In other stories, the key events take place in the minds of the characters. Is this story told more through the characters' thoughts and feelings? Or is it told more through their outward actions?

My Fair Neighbor

1. What is the title of this story? Can you think of another good title?

2. Is there a character in this story who makes you think of yourself or someone you know? What did the character say or do to make you think that?

3. An author builds the plot around the conflict in a story. In this story, what forces or characters are struggling against each other? How is the conflict finally resolved?

The Auspicious Vision

1. Good writing always has an effect on the reader. How did you feel when you finished reading this story? Were you surprised, horrified, amused, sad, touched, or inspired? What elements in the story made you feel that way?

2. Interesting story plots often have unexpected twists and turns. What surprises did you find in this story?

3. Which character in this story do you most admire? Why? Which character do you like the least?

Thinking About
the Book

1. Choose your favorite illustration in this book. Use this picture as a springboard to write a new story. Give the characters different names. Begin your story with something they are saying or thinking.

2. Compare the stories in this book. Which was the most interesting? Why? In what ways were they alike? In what ways different?

3. Good writers usually write about what they know best. If you wrote a story, what kind of characters would you create? What would be the setting?